Original
Low Point
Recipes

From
Members and Leaders

Edited by Sue Ashworth

SIMON & SCHUSTER

A VIACOM COMPANY

First published in Great Britain by Simon and Schuster, 1999
A Viacom Company

Simon and Schuster UK Ltd
Africa House
64-78 Kingsway
London
WC2B 6SX

Weight Watchers and *123 Success 2000* are Trademarks of Weight Watchers
International, Inc. and used under its control by Weight Watchers (U.K.) Ltd.

Design: Moore Lowenhoff
Front cover design: Design in Mind
Typesetting: Stylize Digital Artwork
Photography: Steve Lee
Styling: Marian Price
Food preparation: Sara Lewis

Weight Watchers Publications Manager: Elizabeth Egan
Weight Watchers Publications Assistant: Celia Whiston

A CIP catalogue record is available from the British Library

ISBN 0 684 85182 2

Printed in Hong Kong.

Recipe notes:
Egg size is medium, unless otherwise stated.
Fruit and vegetables are medium-sized, unless otherwise stated.
It is important to use proper measuring spoons, not cutlery, for spoon measures.
1 tablespoon = 15 ml; 1 teaspoon = 5 ml.
Dried herbs can be substituted for fresh ones, but the flavour may not always be as
good. Halve the fresh-herb quantity stated in the recipe.

Ⓥ shows the recipe is suitable for vegetarians

Contents

Introduction

Congratulations to all the contributors to this unique Weight Watchers cookbook. We knew that if we asked you for some innovative recipes, you would come up with the goods. We have recognised for some time that your ideas would be worth going into print – and here's the result. Now so many of us will be able to share the enjoyment of these delicious winning recipes. Thank you!

In a special competition, we asked Members and Leaders of Weight Watchers to submit favourite Low-Point recipes which they had created themselves. They were to fall into one of three sections – Light Meals, Main Meals or Desserts and Cakes. We were overwhelmed with the response – literally hundreds of you wrote in with a bounty of delicious recipes, posing a very tricky problem for the judges. Just how do you whittle down the entries to provide 30 winners? Not an easy task – but a very enjoyable one!

We hope that you will enjoy the recipes we have chosen. We wanted to provide a good range of recipes which would easily fit into today's busy lifestyles. We looked for recipes without too much preparation and without too many different or expensive ingredients. We also wanted to reflect modern ideas about food and cookery so we looked for dishes with a light and healthy approach. But because we all enjoy treats, there is a handful of indulgent recipes too.

As you know, with the wonderful Weight Watchers *123 Success 2000 Programme*, you can eat anything you like, as long as you count the Points towards your daily total. Within this framework there is plenty of scope for interest and innovation and it is wonderful to see how you have developed some fabulous food – low in fat and Calories, yet full of flavour. It was also exciting to read your stories of success with Weight Watchers. So many of you are Gold or Lifetime Members, following the Programme to maintain Goal.

We know that Weight Watchers recipe books help you to achieve this by providing interesting food to keep you satisfied. Enjoying your food helps to boost morale and these recipes will provide even more ways to keep you on track. Because the recipes are all from fellow Weight Watchers Members, you can be sure that they have been tried and tested to produce tasty and slimming results. And the marvellous thing is that these dishes don't taste like 'slimming' food – they simply taste delicious – because they are wholesome, satisfying and home-made.

Sue Ashworth

November 1998

Light Meals

Weight Watchers Members and Leaders are very creative when it comes to cooking up something exciting and it's great to see such a wide range of foods being used so creatively. Whether you want quick and easy snacks and suppers or something a little more complicated, you're sure to find something to suit your tastes in this chapter of delicious light meals.

Boredom can often pose a threat to a diet, but these recipes are guaranteed to keep your palate interested until you reach your Goal. And for those who have already achieved that aim, they will help to keep you there.

Pasta with Green Beans and Sun-dried Tomatoes

Alex is a Gold Member who loves cooking and creating new recipes. You'll love her tasty pasta recipe – it's healthy, quick, and satisfying. Serve with a green salad.

Alex Smith, Bicester, Oxfordshire   Meeting: Bicester, Oxfordshire

Serves: 2
Preparation time: 5 minutes + 10 minutes cooking
Freezing: not recommended
Points per serving: 5
Total Points per recipe: 10
Calories per serving: 195

Ⓥ

175 g (6 oz) pasta shapes
175 g (6 oz) fine green beans, sliced
1 tablespoon green or red pesto sauce
85 g (3 oz) low-fat soft cheese
55 g (2 oz) sun-dried tomatoes, rinsed and
**   patted dry**
salt and freshly ground black pepper
basil leaves, to garnish (optional)

❶ Cook the pasta in plenty of lightly salted boiling water for about 8–10 minutes until just tender.
❷ Meanwhile, steam or boil the green beans for about 5 minutes, until cooked.
❸ Drain the pasta and add the beans with the pesto sauce and soft cheese, stirring to mix. Add the sun-dried tomatoes, then season with a little salt and pepper.

❹ Serve, scattered with a few fresh basil leaves.

Cook's tip: when you buy fresh basil, avoid storing it in the fridge since the leaves will blacken in the cold.

Variation: use mange-tout or sugar snap peas instead of fine green beans.

Cheese and Ham Bake (page 12)

Warm Salad of Turkey Rashers with Blue Cheese

Turkey rashers are very versatile and in this recipe Kareen uses them to great advantage in a tasty, warm salad with new potatoes and blue cheese.

Kareen Horne, Peterhead, Aberdeenshire   Meeting: Peterhead

Serves: 4

Preparation time: 10 minutes + 20 minutes cooking

Freezing: not recommended

Points per serving: 3¹/₂

Total Points per recipe: 14

Calories per serving: 190

450 g (1 lb) new potatoes, scrubbed and diced
low-fat cooking spray
200 g (7 oz) turkey rashers, cut into pieces
6 spring onions, chopped finely
mixed salad leaves
12 cherry tomatoes, halved
55 g (2 oz) Danish blue cheese, crumbled
salt and freshly ground black pepper
chopped fresh chives or parsley, to garnish

❶ Cook the potatoes in lightly salted boiling water until tender, about 15 minutes.

❷ Spray a non-stick frying-pan 2 or 3 times with the cooking spray. Add the turkey rashers and cook, stirring, for 2–3 minutes.

❸ Add the potatoes and spring onions and cook for 2–3 minutes to heat through. Season with salt and pepper.

❹ Arrange the salad leaves on 4 serving plates with the cherry tomatoes. Pile the potato mixture into the middle, then sprinkle with the blue cheese. Sprinkle each serving with chopped fresh chives or parsley, then serve.

Cook's tip: use leftover boiled or jacket potatoes in the recipe instead of new ones and omit step 1.

Variation: add a tablespoon of fat-free vinaigrette dressing to each portion just before serving, or try a blue cheese dressing, remembering to add the necessary Points.

Mixed Mushroom Risotto

Ideal for vegetarians, Sue's recipe can be adjusted to suit your own tastes so feel free to mix and match your favourite vegetables.

Sue Coats, Appleton, Warrington, Cheshire   Meeting: Woolston, Lymm, Cheshire

Serves: 2

Preparation time: 10 minutes + 25 minutes cooking

Freezing: not recommended

Points per serving: 2

Total Points per recipe: 4

Calories per serving: 225

Ⓥ

low-fat cooking spray

350 g (12 oz) mixed mushrooms (e.g. button, oyster, shiitake or chestnut mushrooms), sliced

1 red pepper, de-seeded and chopped

1 green pepper, de-seeded and chopped

1 celery stick, chopped

1 leek, sliced

1 garlic clove, crushed

85 g (3 oz) arborio (risotto) rice

1/2 teaspoon dried mixed herbs

2 vegetable stock cubes, dissolved in 850 ml (1 1/2 pints) hot water

salt and freshly ground black pepper

❶ Spray a large saucepan 3 or 4 times with the cooking spray. Add the mushrooms, peppers, celery, leek and garlic. Cover and cook over a low heat for 5 minutes to 'sweat' the vegetables.

❷ Add the rice to the saucepan and cook, stirring, for 1 minute.

❸ Add the dried herbs to the hot stock, then ladle the stock into the saucepan a little at a time. Keep adding hot stock, cooking and stirring between each addition, until it has all been absorbed and the rice is swollen, creamy and tender. This will take about 20 minutes.

❹ Season to taste and then spoon the risotto on to warm serving plates and serve at once.

Cook's tip: to make sure that the risotto is rich and creamy, make sure that you use the correct rice which is called 'arborio'.

Variation: if you're not a vegetarian, add 175 g (6 oz) chopped, cooked chicken to the risotto 5 minutes before the end of cooking time for a more substantial meal and use chicken stock cubes instead of vegetable ones. The Points per serving will be 4.

Mixed Leaf, Raisin and Almond Salad

Rosemary finds this colourful salad very versatile – she either takes it to work for lunch with some bread or serves it as a side dish with pasta or low-fat ready meals.

Rosemary Woodland, Leicester   Meeting: Scraptoft Village Hall, Leicestershire

Serves: 4
Preparation time: 10 minutes
Freezing: not recommended
Points per serving: 1
Total Points per recipe: 4¹/₂
Calories per serving: 115

Ⓥ

4 spring onions, chopped
2 tomatoes, chopped
2 large handfuls of mixed salad leaves, e.g.
    frisée, lamb's lettuce, radicchio, chopped
6 sprigs of fresh coriander, chopped
1 crisp eating apple, chopped
55 g (2 oz) seedless grapes, halved
4 teaspoons flaked almonds
2 heaped tablespoons raisins
100 g (3¹/₂ oz) canned sweetcorn, drained
    and rinsed
2 tablespoons fat-free vinaigrette dressing
salt and freshly ground black pepper

❶ In a salad bowl, mix together the spring onions, tomatoes, salad leaves, coriander, apple and grapes. Stir in the almonds and raisins.

❷ Add the sweetcorn. Season with a little salt and pepper.

❸ Just before serving, add the vinaigrette dressing and then toss the ingredients together.

Cook's tips: you can buy ready-prepared packets of mixed salad leaves in the supermarket which save time and money.

Adding the vinaigrette dressing just before serving ensures that the ingredients remain crisp.

Variation: you can add other salad vegetables – such as celery or beansprouts – without adding Points.

Warm Salad of Turkey Rashers with Blue Cheese (page 8)
Mixed Mushroom Risotto (page 9)

Cheese and Ham Bake

Thanks to the Weight Watchers Programme, Sheila has returned to her Goal Weight. Try one of her favourite recipes for success – it's quick, easy and economical. Serve with a mixed salad (remember – it's Point-free!).

Sheila Thomas, Blackpool, Lancashire   Meeting: St. Mary's Church, Blackpool, Lancashire

Serves: 1
Preparation time: 10 minutes + 40 minutes cooking
Freezing: recommended (see Cook's tips)
Points per serving: 6
Total Points per recipe: 6
Calories per serving: 230

2 potatoes, cut into chunks
1/2 onion, chopped finely
2 tablespoons plain cottage cheese
25 g (1 oz) cooked ham, chopped
1 tablespoon mature Cheddar cheese, grated
1 tomato, sliced
salt and freshly ground black pepper

1 Preheat the oven to Gas Mark 6/200°C/400°F.
2 Cook the potatoes and onion in lightly salted boiling water for about 20 minutes, until tender.
3 Drain the potatoes and mash them with the cottage cheese. Stir in the chopped ham and season with salt and pepper.
4 Put the potato mixture into an individual ovenproof dish. Top with the grated cheese and sliced tomato. Bake for about 15–20 minutes, until the cheese is melted and golden brown.

Cook's tips: this is a good way to use up leftover mashed potato.
 If freezing, leave out the tomato until re-heating.

Variation: replace the ham with 100 g (3 1/2 oz) of tuna fish in brine (well drained). The Points will remain the same.

Country Veg Omelette

Filling, tasty and nutritious, it's hard to believe that Corinne's delicious omelette recipe is so low in Points. Serve with a green salad and some extra Point-free vegetables.

Corrine Coull, Redhouse, Sunderland   Meeting: St. Cuthbert's, Redhouse

Serves: 2
Preparation time: 10 minutes + 15 minutes cooking
Freezing: not recommended
Points per serving: 2 1/2
Total Points per recipe: 5 1/2
Calories per serving: 205

Ⓥ

40 g (1 1/2 oz) pasta shapes, e.g. fusilli, macaroni or farfalle
1 teaspoon vegetable oil
115 g (4 oz) finely sliced vegetables, e.g. courgette, red or yellow peppers, leek, red onion
2 eggs, beaten
2 tablespoons skimmed milk
1/4 teaspoon mixed dried herbs
salt and freshly ground black pepper

1 Cook the pasta in lightly salted boiling water for 8–10 minutes, or according to the pack instructions.
2 Meanwhile, heat the oil in a non-stick omelette pan and stir-fry the vegetables for 3–4 minutes until softened.
3 Drain the pasta and add to the vegetables. Beat the eggs, milk and mixed herbs together, season with salt and pepper, then pour into the omelette pan.

4 Cook over a gentle heat until the eggs are set and then slice the omelette in half to serve.

Cook's tip: this is an excellent recipe for using up any leftover cooked pasta.

Variation: try using a flavoured olive oil to make this omelette even tastier. Rosemary, basil or garlic-flavoured oils would be ideal.

Aubergine Bake

You can't get lower than 0 Points per serving for a Weight Watchers recipe, so enjoy Trizie's amazing vegetable bake as often as you like!

Trizie Hodge, Cardiff, South Wales   Meeting: Llanishen

Serves: 1
Preparation time: 10 minutes + 30 minutes cooking
Freezing: not recommended
Points per serving: 0
Total Points per recipe: 0
Calories per serving: 110

Ⓥ

1 aubergine
1 small red onion, chopped
2 garlic cloves, chopped
400 g (14 oz) canned chopped tomatoes
a pinch of ground cumin
a pinch of ground coriander
salt and freshly ground black pepper

1 Preheat the oven to Gas Mark 4/180°C/350°F.
2 Slice the aubergine lengthways, without cutting it all the way through, so that it can be fanned out from the stalk end. Place it in a shallow ovenproof dish.
3 Mix together the onion and garlic and sprinkle them between the aubergine slices. Drain off a little juice from the tomatoes, then pour the tomatoes over the aubergine. Season with the cumin, coriander, salt and pepper.

4 Cover the baking dish with a lid or a piece of foil. Transfer to the oven and cook for approximately 30 minutes, removing the lid or foil for the last 10 minutes to dry the bake out a little.

Cook's tip: serve the bake on its own, or as a side dish.

Variation: try using chopped tomatoes flavoured with basil or herbs.

Caribbean Chicken

Wendy is a Leader from Rossett in North Wales. Over the years she has shared this recipe with many of her Members, and now we can all enjoy it.

Wendy Williams, Rossett, Wrexham, North Wales   Meeting: Wendy runs 11 Meetings in the Wrexham area

Serves: 2
Preparation time: 10 minutes
Freezing: not recommended
Points per serving: $4^1/_2$
Total Points per recipe: $8^1/_2$
Calories per serving: 275

150 g ($5^1/_2$ oz) cooked long-grain rice
4 pineapple rings in natural juice, chopped and juice reserved
2 teaspoons desiccated coconut
100 g ($3^1/_2$ oz) seedless grapes, halved
$^1/_4$ red pepper, de-seeded and chopped
$^1/_4$ yellow pepper, de-seeded and chopped
4 spring onions, chopped
4 cherry tomatoes, quartered
1 celery stick, chopped
1 medium cooked skinless, boneless chicken breast, diced
1–2 Chinese leaves or crisp lettuce leaves, shredded
salt and freshly ground black pepper

1 Mix together the cooked rice, chopped pineapple, coconut, grapes, peppers, spring onions, tomatoes, celery and chicken. Season with a little salt and pepper.

2 Divide the mixture between 2 serving plates and garnish with the shredded Chinese leaves or lettuce leaves.

3 Sprinkle 2 tablespoons of pineapple juice over each portion, then serve. Alternatively, cover and refrigerate for up to four hours.

Cook's tips: why not pack up a portion to take to work for lunch? Remember to keep it chilled.

Variation: this is ideal for buffets and at Christmas when you can simply replace the chicken with any leftover turkey.

Spicy Tortilla

Lesley finds that this light meal redresses the balance when she has gone a little overboard earlier in the day.

Lesley Brown, Bow, London   Meeting: Bethnal Green

Serves: 1

Preparation time: 5 minutes + 5 minutes cooking

Freezing: not recommended

Points per serving: 4

Total Points per recipe: 4

Calories per serving: 240

Ⓥ

$1/2$ **small red onion, chopped finely**

4 button mushrooms, halved

6 cherry tomatoes, halved

1 garlic clove, chopped finely

$1/4$ **teaspoon chilli powder**

1 medium-size flour tortilla

$1/2$ **bunch of watercress**

2 tablespoons reduced-fat hummous

salt and freshly ground black pepper

1 Put the onion, mushrooms, tomatoes, garlic and chilli powder into a small non-stick frying-pan. Add a small amount of water and cook, stirring, for about 3–4 minutes.

2 Meanwhile, warm the tortilla under the grill. Transfer to a large plate and arrange the watercress on top, then spoon on the cooked vegetable mixture. Top with the hummous, then season with salt and pepper.

3 Roll up the tortilla and serve.

Variations: use a handful of baby spinach leaves instead of the watercress.

Instead of a tortilla, use pitta bread or a bread roll. A medium-size pitta bread will increase the Points by $1/2$.

Lemon and Mint Prawn Salad (page 19)
Citrus Scallops (page 18)

Citrus Scallops

Ann adores good food and cooking, and loves to create low-fat alternatives to dishes she tries out in restaurants. This one is perfect for a light meal or starter. The flavours are exquisite.

Ann Hopton, Gerrards Cross, Buckinghamshire
Meeting: A Leader for 10 years, Ann currently takes 3 Meetings.

Serves: 2
Preparation time: 10 minutes + 30 minutes marinating + 10 minutes cooking
Freezing: not recommended
Points per serving: 2
Total Points per recipe: 4$^{1}/_{2}$
Calories per serving: 100

juice and rind of 2 limes
1 or 2 teaspoons finely grated fresh root ginger
1 garlic clove, crushed
1 shallot, chopped finely
175 g (6 oz) king scallops (about 6)
olive oil spray
25 g (1 oz) slice of Parma ham, cut into thin strips
1 or 2 teaspoons fish sauce or light soy sauce
chopped fresh chives, to garnish

❶ Mix together the lime juice, ginger, garlic and shallot in a shallow dish. Remove the corals from the scallops and add to the lime juice mixture. Slice the scallops in half horizontally and add them too. Stir, cover and leave to marinate for at least 30 minutes.

❷ Drain the scallops, reserving the marinade. Heat a non-stick frying-pan or wok and spray 2 or 3 times with the olive oil spray. Add the scallops and cook over a high heat, stirring, for 2–3 minutes. Transfer to warmed plates.

❸ Add the Parma ham to the frying-pan or wok, cook over a high heat for 1 or 2 minutes and then scatter over the scallops.

❹ Add the marinade to the pan or wok with the fish sauce or soy sauce, bring to the boil and then pour it over the scallops and ham. Season with a little salt and pepper, then serve, garnished with the lime rind and chopped fresh chives.

Cooks tip: fish sauce is a thin, dark, salty liquid available from most supermarkets and delicatessens. You'll find it among the oriental products, especially the Thai foods.

For a special occasion, serve the scallops in radicchio leaves with a few sprigs of watercress.

Variation: if fresh chives are unavailable, use a couple of finely sliced spring onions.

Lemon and Mint Prawn Salad

As a Weight Watchers Leader, Nina-Louise loves to try out low-fat alternatives to favourite recipes.
This is her winning recipe for a starter.

Nina-Louise McKerlie, Forest Park, Bracknell, Berkshire
Meeting: Nina-Louise takes 3 Meetings in Bracknell, Berkshire.

Serves: 4
Preparation time: 10 minutes
Freezing: not recommended
Points per serving: 2
Total Points per recipe: 8$^1/_2$
Calories per serving: 145

juice of 1 lemon
2 tablespoons low-fat plain yogurt
1 teaspoon mayonnaise
1 teaspoon mint sauce concentrate
1 teaspoon white wine vinegar
mixed salad leaves, shredded
225 g (8 oz) cooked, peeled prawns, defrosted if frozen
salt and freshly ground black pepper
To serve:
chopped fresh chives (optional)
4 lemon wedges
4 medium slices of wholemeal bread
a pinch of paprika

1 To make the dressing, put the lemon juice, yogurt, mayonnaise, mint sauce and vinegar into a screw-top jar. Season with salt and pepper, then shake well to mix.

2 Arrange the shredded salad leaves on serving plates or in 4 attractive glasses. Divide the prawns evenly between them.

3 Drizzle the dressing over the prawns, sprinkle with a few fresh chives, if using, and garnish with lemon wedges and a sprinkling of paprika. Serve each portion with a slice of bread cut into triangles.

Variation: try a lime and ginger combination for the dressing by using the juice of 1 lime instead of a lemon. Use 1 teaspoon of finely grated fresh root ginger instead of the mint sauce.

Main Meals

Weight Watchers Members and Leaders have come up with some cracking good recipes for meals. In this chapter you'll find lots of ideas for dinner which are sure to lighten up your life. Not only are they easy to put together, they're easy on your waistline too.

Whether you're looking for new ideas for meals with meat or fish or just some inspirational vegetarian dishes, you'll find plenty of suggestions in this chapter. What's more, by cooking these delicious dishes, you know you'll be putting healthy meals on the table which the whole family can enjoy.

One Pot Pork

Elaine developed this recipe from a one-pot meal her mother used to make when they went on caravan holidays as children. Weight Watchers Members can enjoy it too. It's delicious with rice, potatoes and pasta – just remember to add the extra Points.

Elaine Watson, Earlswood, Chepstow   Meeting: The George, Chepstow

Serves: 2
Preparation time: 10 minutes + 45 minutes cooking
Freezing: recommended
Points per serving: 4
Total Points per recipe: 7¹/₂
Calories per serving: 330

350 g (12 oz) pork tenderloin (fillet), cut into
   thin strips
1 pork or chicken stock cube dissolved in
   300 ml (¹/₂ pint) water
¹/₂ teaspoon dry mustard
¹/₄ teaspoon ground ginger
1 tablespoon tomato purée
1 large leek, sliced finely
115 g (4 oz) mushrooms, sliced
1 cooking apple, peeled and sliced
paprika, to garnish
salt and freshly ground black pepper

❶ Dry-fry the pork in a large non-stick saucepan for about 3–4 minutes, until sealed.
❷ Mix the pork or chicken stock with the mustard, ginger and tomato purée. Add to the saucepan and bring to the boil. Add the leek, mushrooms and cooking apple. Cover and simmer for 20–25 minutes.
❸ Season to taste and sprinkle with paprika to garnish.

Cook's tips: the cooking time may need to be increased if cheaper cuts of meat such as leg of pork are used.

Add some extra 'free' vegetables such as carrots or broccoli in step 2 if you want the recipe to serve four people.

Lamb Dopiaza (Spicy Lamb Stew)

Colleen loves Indian food but it is often very high in Points, so she devised this delicious low-Point lamb curry.
Serve with chunks of crusty bread, rice or poppadoms, remembering to add the extra Points.

Colleen Cooper, Coalville, Leicestershire   Meeting: Coalville

Serves: 4

Preparation time: 10 minutes + 1 hour 40 minutes
cooking

Freezing: recommended

Points per serving: 3¹/₂

Total Points per recipe: 15

Calories per serving: 195

---

low-fat cooking spray

**400 g (14 oz) lean lamb, cut into 2.5 cm
(1 inch) cubes**

2 onions, sliced

2 bay leaves

**2.5 cm (1 inch) piece of root ginger, peeled and
chopped**

4 garlic cloves, peeled and chopped

1 teaspoon ground coriander

¹/₂ teaspoon ground cumin

¹/₂ teaspoon ground turmeric

100 g (3¹/₂ oz) low-fat plain fromage frais

¹/₂ teaspoon chilli powder

salt and freshly ground black pepper

To garnish (optional):

tomato wedges

sliced red onion

coriander leaves

---

1 Spray a large saucepan 4 or 5 times with the low-fat cooking spray. Add the lamb, onions and bay leaves and cook gently until browned, about 5 minutes.

2 Mix the ginger, garlic, coriander, cumin and turmeric into the low-fat fromage frais. Add to the saucepan, stirring. Add the chilli powder and season with salt and pepper, to taste.

3 Add 350 ml (12 fl oz) hot water to the saucepan. Cover and lower the heat, then simmer for 1¹/₂ hours,

or until the meat is tender and the spicy sauce is thickened. If you wish, garnish each plate with some tomato wedges, sliced red onion and coriander leaves.

Cook's tips: add chilli powder according to taste – a little less if you're not keen on very spicy food, a little more if you like things fiery.

This is suitable for reheating in the microwave.

Savoury Quorn Mince with Sweet Potato and Cheese Topping

Linda's excellent vegetarian recipe is a hit with non-vegetarians too since it's filling and delicious!

Linda Briar, Elland, Halifax, West Yorkshire   Meeting: Greetland, Halifax

Serves: 4

Preparation time: 10 minutes + 35–40 minutes
cooking

Freezing: not recommended

Points per serving: 3

Total Points per recipe: 11

Calories per serving: 190

Ⓥ

2 sweet potatoes, peeled and sliced thinly
low-fat cooking spray
1 onion, chopped finely
1 red pepper, de-seeded and chopped finely
1 yellow pepper, de-seeded and chopped finely
2 garlic cloves, crushed
115 g (4 oz) mushrooms, sliced
300 g (10¹/₂ oz) Quorn mince
400 g (14 oz) canned chopped tomatoes
300 ml (¹/₂ pint) vegetable stock
1 teaspoon mixed dried herbs
2 tablespoons tomato purée
40 g (1¹/₂ oz) low-fat Cheddar-type cheese, grated
salt and freshly ground black pepper

❶ Preheat the oven to Gas Mark 6/200°C/400°F.

❷ Blanch the sweet potatoes in boiling water for
5 minutes.

❸ Spray a large frying-pan or wok 4 or 5 times with
the low-fat cooking spray. Add the onion, peppers
and garlic and cook, stirring for 2–3 minutes. Add
the mushrooms and Quorn mince and cook for a
further 2–3 minutes.

❹ Stir in the chopped tomatoes, stock, mixed herbs
and tomato purée. Season with salt and pepper.
Bring to the boil, then remove from the heat.

❺ Transfer the mixture into a 2 litre (3¹/₂ pint)
casserole dish. Arrange the sliced sweet potatoes
on top and sprinkle with grated cheese. Bake in the
oven for 20–25 minutes, or until the cheese has
melted and turned golden brown.

Cook's tip: to prevent the sweet potatoes from going
black, don't peel them until you are ready to par-boil
them and then add a few drops of lemon juice to the
boiling water.

Tropical Turkey Steaks (page 30)
Savoury Quorn Mince with Sweet Potato
and Cheese Topping

Pasta Rustica

Mikailia is a Weight Watchers Gold Member. She invented this easy pasta recipe when she had a lot of fresh mushrooms and a surge of creative energy.

Mikailia Bishop, Southbourne, Hampshire   Meeting: Emsworth, Hampshire

Serves: 4
Preparation time: 10 minutes + 30 minutes cooking
Freezing: not recommended
Points per serving: 5$^1/_2$
Total Points per recipe: 22$^1/_2$
Calories per serving: 430

Ⓥ

2 large Spanish onions, chopped finely
450 g (1 lb) mixed mushrooms (chestnut, button, oyster, etc.) chopped
400 g (14 oz) canned chopped tomatoes
8 medium turkey rashers, chopped
2 garlic cloves, crushed
2 teaspoons pesto sauce
200 g (7 oz) fat-free Greek-style plain yogurt
280 g (10 oz) pasta shapes
salt and freshly ground black pepper
To garnish:
4 teaspoons finely grated parmesan cheese
fresh basil leaves

❶ Place the onions, mushrooms, tomatoes, turkey rashers, garlic and pesto sauce in a large saucepan or large frying-pan with a lid. Bring to the boil, then reduce the heat. Cover and simmer for 20 minutes.

❷ Remove the lid and allow the sauce to reduce and thicken for a few minutes. Add the yogurt, stirring to mix, then season to taste with salt and pepper.

❸ Meanwhile, cook the pasta in plenty of lightly salted boiling water for about 8–10 minutes, or according to pack instructions.

❹ Drain the pasta well, stir through the sauce, then divide between 4 warm serving plates. Sprinkle each portion with a teaspoon of parmesan cheese, then serve, garnished with basil leaves.

Cook's tips: leave out the turkey rashers if you are a vegetarian. The Points per serving will be 4$^1/_2$.

Fresh basil leaves are available in most supermarkets and add a delicious finishing touch to pasta dishes.

Pasta Rustica
Mediterranean Fish Ragout (page 30)

Kimberley Chicken

Now everyone will be able to enjoy Val's truly inspired recipe for chicken. As this recipe shows, she loves good food and enjoys trying out new combinations.

Valmai Stephens, Caerphilly, Mid Glamorgan, Wales   Meeting: Caerphilly

Serves: 4

Preparation time: 20 minutes + 45 minutes cooking

Freezing: not recommended

Points per serving: 4

Total Points per recipe: 16

Calories per serving: 235

low-fat cooking spray
4 spring onions, chopped finely
1 red, green or yellow pepper, de-seeded and chopped
115 g (4 oz) mushrooms, sliced
2 teaspoons mixed dried herbs
4 medium skinless, boneless chicken breasts
4 small low-fat cheese triangles
2 teaspoons tomato purée
2 teaspoons garlic purée
2 teaspoons ground coriander
400 g (14 oz) canned chopped tomatoes, pushed through a sieve
225 g (8 oz) fresh spinach
4 teaspoons low-fat plain fromage frais or low-fat plain yogurt
1 packet of Jordan's cheese & chives crisps (98% fat free), crushed
salt and freshly ground black pepper
parsley sprigs or a few mixed dried herbs, to garnish

① Preheat the oven to Gas Mark 4/180°C/350°F.

② Spray a large frying-pan 4 or 5 times with the low-fat cooking spray. Add the spring onions, pepper, mushrooms and mixed herbs. Cook, stirring, for 4–5 minutes, then remove from the heat and transfer to a dish. Season with salt and pepper.

③ Cut a pocket into each chicken breast using a sharp knife. Fill each one with some of the cooked vegetables and a cheese triangle. Secure each with a long wooden skewer or satay stick.

④ Brown the chicken breasts on both sides in the frying-pan, then transfer to a casserole dish. Add the remaining vegetables to the frying-pan with the tomato purée, garlic purée, coriander and tomatoes. Bring to the boil, reduce the heat and simmer until reduced by half. Add to the chicken in the casserole dish, cover and bake for 45 minutes.

⑤ Five minutes before the end of cooking time, cook the spinach in a very small amount of lightly salted boiling water. Drain well and spoon on to 4 warm serving plates.

⑥ Place a chicken breast on top of each pile of spinach, spoon the sauce over and top with fromage frais or yogurt and crushed crisps. Garnish with parsley sprigs or a sprinkling of mixed dried herbs, then serve.

Cook's tips: you can buy sieved Italian tomatoes – called passata – instead of having to push the canned tomatoes through a sieve yourself.

Use a mixture of red, green and yellow peppers if you can, to add lots of colour.

Tropical Turkey Steaks

Just the ticket for an easy lunch or supper dish, Christine's recipe has all the necessary elements for success. Serve with new potatoes, baby corn and green beans, remembering to add the Points as necessary.

Christine Morris, Wallasey, Merseyside   Meeting: New Brighton, Wirral, Merseyside

Serves: 2
Preparation time: 10 minutes + 25 minutes cooking
Freezing: not recommended
Points per serving: 7
Total Points per recipe: 14
Calories per serving: 330

$1/2$ teaspoon vegetable oil
2 x 100 g ($3^1/2$ oz) turkey breast steaks
2 slices canned pineapple rings in natural juice
4 medium turkey rashers
100 g ($3^1/2$ oz) half-fat Cheddar-type cheese, grated
salt and freshly ground black pepper

1 Preheat the oven to Gas Mark 4/180°C/350°F. Lightly grease a shallow baking dish with the oil.

2 Put the turkey steaks into the baking dish and put a pineapple ring on top of each one. Fold each turkey rasher in half or pleat it into 3 parts and put two rashers on top of each turkey steak. Sprinkle with grated cheese. Season with salt and pepper.

3 Put the lid on the dish or cover with foil. Bake for 15–20 minutes, then remove the lid and continue to cook for a further 5 minutes, or until the cheese has browned slightly.

Cook's tip: sprinkle the turkey steaks with a shake of paprika or cayenne pepper if you want to add some spice.

Variation: skinless, boneless chicken breasts could be used instead of turkey steaks.

Mediterranean Fish Ragout

Perfect for all the family to enjoy, Stephanie's recipe is full of fabulous flavours. Serve with plain boiled rice, noodles or pasta, remembering to add the extra Points.

Stephanie Pattle, Great Linford, Milton Keynes   Meeting: Neath Hill, Milton Keynes

Serves: 4
Preparation time: 15 minutes + 50 minutes cooking time
Freezing: not recommended
Points per serving: $1^1/2$
Total Points per recipe: $6^1/2$
Calories per serving: 190

1 teaspoon olive oil
1 large onion, sliced
1 garlic clove, crushed
1 green pepper, de-seeded and sliced
1 yellow pepper, de-seeded and sliced
4×115 g (4 oz) cod fillets, skinned and cut into chunks
400 g (14 oz) canned chopped tomatoes
175 g (6 oz) mushrooms, halved
1 small courgette, sliced
10 olives, pitted and halved
2 teaspoons dried basil
125 ml (4 fl oz) glass of white wine
salt and freshly ground black pepper

① Preheat the oven to Gas Mark 6/200°C/400°F.
② Heat the oil in a large frying-pan and sauté the onion and garlic until soft, about 3–4 minutes. Add the peppers and cook for a further 2 minutes, stirring constantly.
③ Put the fish chunks into a 1.7 litre (3 pint) casserole dish along with the tomatoes, mushrooms, and courgette. Add the onion, garlic and peppers from the frying-pan, then add the olives, basil and white wine. Season with salt and pepper.
④ Cover the casserole dish, transfer to the oven and bake for 40 minutes.

Simple Salmon

Diana is a Member from Leigh-on-Sea in Essex and this is one of her favourite recipes. It is low in Points, easy to make and very tasty. Serve each portion of fish with a medium jacket potato (add 2¹/₂ Points) or a medium portion of boiled potatoes (add 2 Points).

Diana Barnes, Leigh-on-Sea, Essex   Meeting: Leigh-on-Sea

Serves: 2
Preparation time: 10 minutes + 30 minutes cooking
Freezing: not recommended
Points per serving: 4
Total Points per recipe: 7¹/₂
Calories per serving: 300

2 × 115 g (4 oz) salmon fillets, skinned
2 small leeks, chopped
2 small courgettes, sliced
¹/₂ yellow pepper, de-seeded and sliced
1 tablespoon chopped fresh tarragon
    (or 1 teaspoon dried)
1 tablespoon chopped fresh dill
    (or 1 teaspoon dried)
250 ml (9 fl oz) fresh orange juice
salt and freshly ground black pepper
To garnish (optional):
a few slices of lime
a few sprigs of fresh dill

① Preheat the oven to Gas Mark 6/200°C/400°F.
② Put the salmon fillets into an ovenproof dish measuring about 15 × 20 cm (6 × 8 in). Arrange all the vegetables over the salmon and sprinkle with the tarragon and dill.
③ Pour the orange juice over the fish and vegetables, then season with salt and pepper. Cover the dish with a lid or a piece of foil.

④ Transfer the dish to the oven and bake for 30 minutes. Check halfway through the cooking time and baste the fish with the juices in the dish. If desired, serve garnished with a few slices of lime and some sprigs of fresh dill.

Cook's tip: you can also use cod or haddock fillets instead of salmon. The Points per serving will be 2¹/₂.

Bulgar Wheat and Prawn Risotto

This recipe helped Eileen to achieve her Goal Weight. It's filling, nutritious and easy to make.

Eileen Saunders, Verwood, Dorset   Meeting: Verwood, Dorset

Serves: 2

Preparation time: 15 minutes + 20 minutes cooking

Freezing: not recommended

Points per serving: 3¹/₂

Total Points per recipe: 7¹/₂

Calories per serving: 265

85 g (3 oz) bulgar wheat

1 vegetable stock cube, dissolved in 600 ml (1 pint) hot water

2 spring onions, sliced finely

25 g (1 oz) baby corn

55 g (2 oz) mushrooms, sliced

2 tablespoons frozen peas

25 g (1 oz) green beans, chopped

¹/₂ red pepper, de-seeded and chopped

¹/₂ green pepper, de-seeded and chopped

a pinch of dried tarragon

a pinch of dried dill (optional)

115 g (4 oz) cooked peeled prawns, defrosted if frozen

a few drops of Tabasco sauce (optional)

salt and freshly ground black pepper

To serve:

lemon wedges

a few sprigs of fresh dill

❶ Put the bulgar wheat into a large bowl and cover with boiling water. Allow to soak for about 10 minutes until swollen. Drain well.

❷ Put the bulgar wheat into a large saucepan, frying-pan or wok with the stock, spring onions, baby corn, mushrooms, peas, green beans, peppers, tarragon and dill (if using). Bring up to the boil, then reduce the heat and simmer for about 8 minutes, or until the vegetables are cooked but still slightly crunchy.

❸ When most of the stock has evaporated and the mixture is almost dry, add the prawns. Cook for a further 2–3 minutes to heat them thoroughly.

❹ Season to taste with a few drops of Tabasco pepper sauce and some salt and pepper. Divide between 2 warmed plates and serve at once, garnished with lemon wedges and sprigs of dill.

Cook's tips: to make the dish more substantial, add strips of cooked chicken or beef, and use a chicken or beef stock cube, as appropriate. Remember to add the extra Points.

You can add more Point-free vegetables to the recipe if you wish.

Bulgar Wheat and Prawn Risotto
Simple Salmon (page 31)

Spicy Vegetable Balti Curry

Curries can be very high in fat, Calories and Points – but not this one. Tracey's low-Point recipe is a real winner.

Tracey Curd, Chessington, Surrey   Meeting: Epsom, Surrey

Serves: 4
Preparation time: 15 minutes + 25 minutes cooking
Freezing: recommended
Points per serving: 1
Total Points per recipe: 3
Calories per serving: 110

Ⓥ

1 teaspoon vegetable oil
8 fresh or dried curry leaves (if available)
1 teaspoon mustard seeds
1 teaspoon onion or celery seeds
2 × 400 g (14 oz) canned chopped tomatoes
1 onion, chopped
1 courgette, chopped
1 red pepper, de-seeded and chopped
1 green pepper, de-seeded and chopped
3 garlic cloves, crushed
115 g (4 oz) button mushrooms, halved
1/2 small cauliflower, broken into florets
1 aubergine, cut into chunks
200 g (7 oz) par-boiled potatoes, cut into chunks
1 teaspoon ground coriander
1 teaspoon chilli powder
1 teaspoon ground cumin
1 teaspoon salt
3 tablespoons chopped fresh coriander
a few sprigs of fresh coriander, to garnish
    (optional)

❶ Heat the oil in a large saucepan and add the curry leaves (if using), mustard seeds and onion or celery seeds. Cook for about 1 minute, until the seeds begin to pop.

❷ Add the tomatoes, then all the remaining vegetables. Stir in the ground coriander, chilli powder, cumin and salt. Mix thoroughly.

❸ Cover and cook over a low heat for about 20 minutes, until the potatoes are tender.

❹ Check the seasoning, then serve the curry sprinkled with chopped fresh coriander and garnish with a few sprigs if you wish.

Cook's tips: for a more substantial meal, serve each portion of curry with 4 tablespoons of boiled or steamed rice. This will add 3 Points per serving.

Make a quick raita to serve with the curry by combining 1 small tub of low-fat plain yogurt with 1/2 teaspoon of mint sauce and 5 cm (2 in) piece of chopped cucumber (1/2 Point per serving).

Desserts

I n this chapter you'll find some excellent ideas for delicious puddings and treats. Whether you need a light and lovely recipe to finish off a special meal, or simply want to curl up on the sofa with something indulgent, you'll find what you're looking for here.

Weight Watchers Members love desserts – and why not? The key is to simply keep things in control. By counting the Points and simply fitting them into the wonderful Weight Watchers Programme, you can enjoy treats and still lose weight. So yes, you can eat cake!

Tangy Lemon Cheesecake

Lynn has cleverly adapted this cheesecake recipe for Weight Watchers; it's low in fat, yet creamy and delicious!

Lynn Bustard, Hatfield, Hertfordshire   Meeting: Lord William Cecil Memorial Hall, Hatfield

Serves: 10
Preparation time: 15 minutes + 2 hours chilling
Freezing: recommended
Points per serving: 3
Total Points per recipe: 28$^1/_2$
Calories per serving: 145

15 ginger nuts, crushed
55 g (2 oz) low-fat spread, melted
250 g (9 oz) Quark
250 g (9 oz) low-fat plain fromage frais
4 tablespoons lemon curd
finely grated rind and juice of 1 lemon

Ⓥ

❶ Mix together the crushed ginger nuts and melted low-fat spread. Tip into a 23 cm (9-inch) flan dish and spread out over the base, pressing down well. Chill for 15 minutes.

❷ Beat together the Quark and fromage frais until blended, then add the lemon curd, lemon rind and lemon juice, mixing until smooth.

❸ Pour the mixture over the biscuit base, then transfer to the refrigerator and chill until firm – about 2 hours.

Cook's tips: make 10 individual portions in ramekins or pretty teacups. If you like, you can freeze them – they are delicious served partially frozen.

Variations: for a special touch, decorate with any or all of the following: sliced strawberries, lemon rind curls, blueberries or a sprig of redcurrants. A fine dusting of icing sugar is very pretty – half a teaspoon per plate will do. Add Points as necessary.

Try using digestive biscuits instead of ginger nuts, and 55 g (2 oz) raspberries instead of lemon curd. Points per serving will be 2$^1/_2$.

Exotic Strudel

Filo pastry is luxurious but light and forms the basis of Roberta's fruit-filled creation. She is a Gold Member, and loves to work out new recipes for delicious desserts. Serve the strudel with half-fat crème fraîche, low-fat plain yogurt or fromage frais. Remember to add the extra Points.

Roberta Bloomfield, Henfield, West Sussex Meeting: Penfold Hall, Steyning, West Sussex

Serves: 4

Preparation time: 20 minutes + 15 minutes
chilling + 20–25 minutes cooking

Freezing: not recommended

Points per serving: 4

Total Points per recipe: 16

Calories per serving: 250

Ⓥ

low-fat cooking spray
100 g (3¹/₂ oz) fresh blueberries
1¹/₂ tablespoons molasses sugar
1 mango, peeled and chopped
finely grated rind of 1 lime
50 g (1³/₄ oz) walnuts, chopped
8 sheets of filo pastry, defrosted if frozen

❶ Preheat the oven to Gas Mark 5/190°C/375°F.
Spray a non-stick baking sheet with the low-fat
cooking spray.

❷ Put the blueberries into a non-stick saucepan
with 5 tablespoons of cold water. Heat very gently
until the water boils. Remove from the heat and stir
in the sugar. Allow to cool.

❸ Put the mango, lime rind and walnuts into a
bowl. Add the cooled blueberry mixture and stir
gently. Chill for about 15 minutes to allow the
flavours to blend.

❹ Take one sheet of filo pastry, spray once or twice
with low-fat cooking spray, then cover with a second
sheet. Repeat until there are 4 sheets of pastry on
top of each other.

❺ Spread half the fruit mixture along one long edge
of the pastry, fold in the two short sides, then roll
up from the long edge to enclose the fruit. Place
on to the prepared baking sheet. Repeat with the
remaining filo pastry and filling mixture.

❻ Bake for 20–25 minutes, or until golden brown.
Cut each strudel in two and serve warm.

Cook's tip: keep filo pastry covered to prevent the
sheets from drying out.

Tiramisu

This lovely recipe manages to have all the indulgent qualities of a traditional tiramisu, without the traditional Point value!

Fiona Quinn, Haddenham, Aylesbury, Buckinghamshire
Meeting: Thame Barns Centre, Thame, Oxfordshire

Serves: 4

Preparation time: 10 minutes + 30 minutes chilling

Freezing: not recommended

Points per serving: 3¹/₂

Total Points per recipe: 15

Calories per serving: without liqueur 150;
with liqueur 170

Ⓥ

250 g (9 oz) Quark (low-fat soft cheese)
4 tablespoons low-fat plain yogurt
1 tablespoon caster sugar
¹/₂ teaspoon vanilla essence
125 ml (4¹/₂ fl oz) strong black coffee
2 tablespoons Tia Maria or Kahlua (optional)
16 sponge fingers (boudoir biscuits)
1 teaspoon cocoa powder, for sprinkling

❶ Beat together the Quark, yogurt, caster sugar and vanilla essence to make a smooth cream.

❷ In a separate shallow bowl, mix together the coffee and Tia Maria or Kahlua, if using.

❸ Choose 4 attractive serving glasses or individual dishes. Dip the sponge fingers into the coffee mixture, one at a time, leaving them to soak for 10–20 seconds so that they absorb some of the mixture, without becoming too soggy. Arrange them as you go in 2–3 layers in the glasses or dishes, alternating them with the cream mixture, starting with the biscuits and ending with the cream.

❹ Chill in the refrigerator for at least 30 minutes, then serve, sprinkled with the cocoa powder.

Cook's tips: if you aren't using any alcohol, you will need a couple of extra tablespoons of strong black coffee. This will reduce the Points per serving by ¹/₂.

Variations: you could use Marsala or sweet sherry instead of Tia Maria or Kahlua.

Low-fat soft cheese could be used instead of Quark. This will add 1 Point per serving.

Banana and Malteser Cakes

Jacqueline's low-Point winner is a hit with all of her family – and will be with Weight Watchers Members too!

Jacqueline Mitcheson, Seaton Delaval, Whitley Bay, Tyne & Wear   Meeting: Seaton Delaval

Makes: about 20 cakes
Preparation time: 10 minutes
Freezing: recommended
Points per cake: 1
Total Points per recipe: 22¹/₂
Calories per cake: 65

Ⓥ

210 g packet of low-fat sponge mix
1 egg
1 small banana, mashed
2 × 37 g packets of Maltesers, crushed

❶ Preheat the oven to Gas Mark 6/200°C/400°F.
❷ Make up the sponge mix with the egg according to the pack instructions. Mix in the mashed banana and crushed Maltesers.
❸ Spoon the mixture into 20 cases, then bake in the oven for 10–15 minutes, until risen and golden brown.

❹ Cool on a wire rack.

Cook's tips: use a rolling pin to crush the Maltesers, but avoid crushing them to a powder.
   Only freeze the buns when they are completely cold and use a rigid polythene box. They can be frozen for up to 2 months.

Bananas in Pyjamas

Anna dedicates this quick and easy recipe to her mother, for giving her lots of support and encouragement to lose weight. This is scrumptious served with low-fat vanilla ice cream, low-fat plain yogurt or fromage frais dusted with cinnamon.

Anna Coxall, Letchworth, Hertfordshire   Meeting: St. Michael's Community Centre, Hitchin, Hertfordshire

Serves: 2
Preparation time: 5 minutes + 15–20 minutes cooking
Freezing: not recommended
Points per serving: 6
Total Points per recipe: 11¹/₂
Calories per serving: 245

Ⓥ

2 tablespoons porridge oats
2 tablespoons desiccated coconut
2 medium bananas
2 tablespoons honey

❶ Preheat the oven to Gas Mark 5/190°C/375°F.
❷ Mix the porridge oats and coconut together in a shallow bowl.
❸ Peel the bananas and smear them with the honey, then roll them in the oat mixture. Place in an ovenproof dish, sprinkling any remaining oat mixture over the top.
❹ Bake for 15–20 minutes.

Cook's tip: make sure the bananas aren't too ripe.

Banana and Malteser Cakes
Bananas in Pyjamas

Special Apple Mousse ·

Elaine's lovely apple mousse is light, tangy and refreshing.

Elaine Barber, Compstall, Stockport   Meeting: Romiley Forum, Stockport

Serves: 4

Preparation time: 15 minutes + cooling
  + 2–3 hours chilling

Freezing: not recommended

Points per serving: 5

Total Points per recipe: 21

Calories per serving: 290

Ⓥ

55 g (2 oz) butter
55 g (2 oz) dark brown sugar
300 ml (¹/₂ pint) cooked apple purée
1 teaspoon vanilla essence
¹/₂ teaspoon cinnamon
¹/₂ packet sugar-free jelly crystals
3 tablespoons boiling water
1 egg white
8 tablespoons half-fat crème fraîche

❶ Melt the butter and sugar together in a saucepan, over a very low heat, until the sugar has completely dissolved. Cool completely.

❷ Mix the butter and sugar mixture with the apple purée, vanilla essence and cinnamon.

❸ Dissolve the jelly crystals in the boiling water and stir into the apple mixture.

❹ Beat the egg white in a scrupulously clean bowl until stiff, then fold into the apple mixture with the crème fraîche. Spoon into stemmed glasses and chill for 2–3 hours.

Cook's tips: decorate the desserts with fresh fruit and dust with cinnamon, remembering to add the extra Points of the fruit.

Use any flavour of jelly crystals – strawberry tastes particularly good.

Claret Cup

Sylviane's busy life includes quite a lot of entertaining and she relies on adapted recipes like this one to spoil guests without spoiling her diet.

Sylviane Leaver, Oxted, Surrey   Meeting: Oxted, Surrey

Serves: 8

Preparation time: 10 minutes + cooling
+ 2–3 hours setting

Freezing: not recommended

Points per serving: 1^1/$_2$

Total Points per recipe: 13

Calories per serving: 105

350 ml (12 fl oz) boiling water
2 packets of raspberry-flavoured sugar-free
  jelly crystals
750 ml (25 fl oz) red wine (Claret, preferably)
1 egg white
3 tablespoons caster sugar
100 g (3^1/$_2$ oz) bunch of seedless red grapes

Ⓥ

❶ Pour the boiling water into a bowl and add the 2 packets of jelly crystals, mixing until dissolved. Add the red wine and stir. Cool.

❷ Pour the liquid into 8 stemmed glasses and chill in the refrigerator until set – about 2 or 3 hours.

❸ Beat the egg white in a shallow dish. Put the caster sugar into a separate shallow dish. When the jellies are completely set, dip the rim of each glass into the egg white, and then into the sugar to frost the rim of the glass.

❹ Cut the grapes into bunches of three. Dip into the egg white, then into the sugar to frost them. Allow to dry for a few minutes, arrange on the edges of the glasses to decorate, then serve.

Cook's tip: this recipe is ideal for large gatherings – such as Christmas, New Year and birthday parties.

Sticky Fruit Treat

Debbie often makes these chocolate nibbles in tiny cake cases as a special treat for her friends and family to enjoy.

Debbie Jackson, Nunthorpe, Middlesborough, Cleveland   Meeting: St. Cuthbert's Church, Marton, Cleveland

Serves: 12
Preparation time: 15 minutes
Freezing: not recommended
Points per serving: 3
Total Points per recipe: 37
Calories per serving: 145

Ⓥ

100 g (3¹/₂ oz) dark chocolate
250 g (9 oz) ready-to-eat dried apricots, chopped
250 g (9 oz) ready-to-eat dates, chopped
250 g (9 oz) ready-to-eat dried figs, chopped
1 eating apple, grated
100 g (3¹/₂ oz) glacé cherries, rinsed and chopped

❶ Break the chocolate into pieces and place in a large heatproof bowl. Sit the bowl over a saucepan of gently simmering water to melt the chocolate. Remove from the heat.
❷ Add all the fruit to the chocolate, stirring until coated.
❸ Spoon the mixture into 12 tiny cake cases or spread out in a square cake tin and chill for 1 hour. Cut the square cake into 12 squares to serve.

Cook's tip: if you don't like figs, use seedless raisins instead.
  Don't grate the apple until the moment you need it to prevent it from turning brown.

Deb's Delight

Debbie's favourite dessert combines the three great loves in her life – chocolate, cream and booze! It makes her taste-buds pop, but not the button on her jeans. Enjoy this dessert as an indulgent treat when you feel the need for something chocolately.

Debbie Blackburn, Hull, East Yorkshire   Meeting: Portobello Street Church

Serves: 1
Preparation time: 5 minutes
Freezing: recommended (see Cook's tip)
Points per serving: 8
Total Points per recipe: 8
Calories per serving: 405

Ⓥ

1 small tub of low-fat plain yogurt
1 sachet of chocolate Options drink (Irish Cream flavour)
1 medium banana
1 standard-size Cadbury's Chocolate Flake

❶ Tip the yogurt into a bowl and mix in the sachet of instant chocolate powder.
❷ Chop half the banana and half the chocolate flake and stir into the mixture. Spoon into a glass sundae dish.
❸ Slice the remaining banana and arrange neatly on top of the mixture. Crumble the remaining chocolate flake on top, then serve immediately.

Cook's tip: if freezing, decorate with the sliced banana and chocolate flake when defrosted.

Apricot and Orange Loaf

For a tasty, healthy treat, try a slice of Stella's low-Point fruit cake.

Stella Kehoe-Kelly, Enfield, Middlesex

Meeting: As a Leader, Stella runs 2 Meetings in Enfield Town and Palmers Green

Serves: 10

Preparation time: 15 minutes + 1 hour soaking
+ 1 hour baking

Freezing: recommended

Points per serving: 2

Total Points per recipe: 19^1/$_2$

Calories per serving: 140

200 g (7 oz) ready-to-eat dried apricots, chopped

250 ml (9 fl oz) diluted sugar-free orange squash

low-fat cooking spray

250 g (9 oz) self-raising flour

1 egg

100 g (3^1/$_2$ oz) reduced-Calorie marmalade

Ⓥ

1 Soak the apricots in the orange squash for about 1 hour.

2 Preheat the oven to Gas Mark 4/180°C/350°F. Spray a 900 g (2 lb) loaf tin with low-fat cooking spray, then line with greaseproof paper.

3 Sift the flour into a large bowl. Drain the apricots, reserving the juice. Add the egg, marmalade and apricots to the flour and mix the ingredients together, stirring in enough reserved juice to give a soft, dropping consistency.

4 Spoon the mixture into the prepared tin, then bake for about 1 hour. Test that the cake is cooked by inserting a fine skewer into the centre – it should come out clean. If not, bake the cake for another few minutes.

5 Cool in the tin for about 15 minutes, then transfer to a wire rack to cool completely.

Cook's tip: the cake keeps well for up to a week in an airtight container.

Variation: use a reduced-sugar apricot jam in place of the marmalade, if you prefer. The Points per serving will remain the same.

Tiramisu

Index